DISNEP

抱きしめたい

Everything I Need to Know about Love
I Learned from Disney.

講談社

大切なあなたへ……

To my dearest……

知ってる？
この世界には、誰もが使える
特別な魔法があるんだよ

Did you know that
there's a special kind of magic in this
world that anyone can use?

それは勇気をあげる魔法

It's a magic that gives you courage,

誰かを笑顔にする魔法

...brings a smile to someone's face,

こわばった心を溶かす魔法

...and thaws even
the coldest of hearts.

使ってみたい？
この魔法はとっても簡単

Would you like to try it?
It's really simple.

大切な人をぎゅっと抱きしめるだけ

Just wrap your arms around someone special to you and give them a big hug!

言葉なんていらないよ
すぐに心が通じ合う

*Without saying a word, your hearts
will instantly connect.*

でもこの魔法が

But there are
times when this magic

使えないときもあるんだ
can't be used,

それは
君の心が曇り空のとき
...like when you're feeling
gloomy.

そんなときは思い出して
In those moments,

君を見守る無数の光が
いつも空に広がってること

remember there are always countless stars
shining in the sky, watching over you,

君を大事に思っている人が
いるということ

...people in your life who truly care about you.

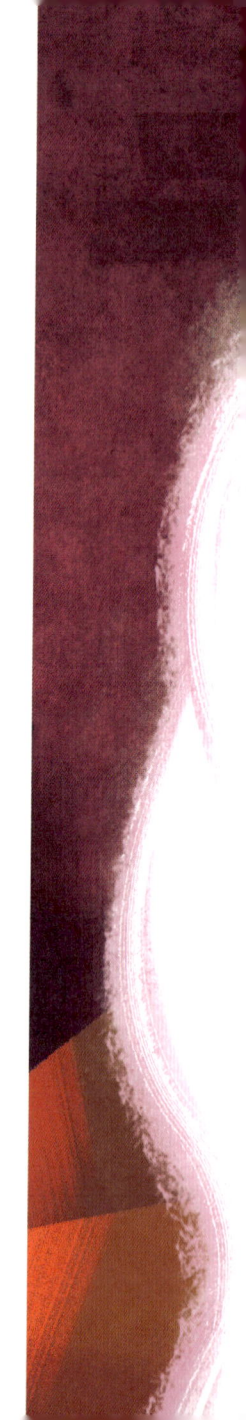

大好きだよ
すぐ泣いちゃう君が

I love you,
even when you're quick to cry.

大好きだよ
おこりんぼうな君が

*I love you,
even when you're feeling
grumpy.*

大好きだよ
はずかしがりやな君が

I love you,
even when you're feeling shy.

君が君のままでいてくれて
とっても嬉しい

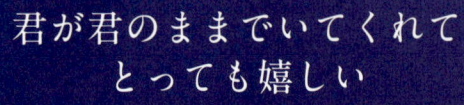

I'm so happy
that you're simply being yourself.

うまくいかない
こともあるけれど

Things won't always go smoothly,

走り続けなくていいんだよ

but you don't have to push yourself to the limit.

いつも頑張ってるの、知ってるから

I know you're
always giving it your all.

失敗したって問題ない

It's okay
to make mistakes.

怒って、泣いて、悔しがって

Let yourself get angry,
cry your heart out, feel the joy!

たくさんの気持ち、経験しよう

Experience all sorts of emotions.

頑張りやさんな君

本当にえらいねって、
ぎゅってしたい

To you,
who always tries so hard…

I want to give you a
big hug and tell you how
amazing you are.

得意なものなんて
なにもない

To you,
who feels down thinking
you're not good
at anything...

そう思って
しょんぼりしてる
君の背中を、
ぎゅってしたい
*I want to
hug you tight.*

君が君でいてくれて
ありがとう

Thank you for being who you are.

I want to wrap my arms
around the miracle that is you.

出会ってくれた奇跡に、
ぎゅってしたい

あの人と比べて
卑屈になっちゃうときがあっても、大丈夫

*When comparing yourself to others
has you feeling down, it's okay.*

気づいてないだけで、ほら

You may not have noticed,
but look!

君だけの素晴らしい宝物が
きらめいている

You have a unique treasure
that shines brightly.

疲れちゃったら、ひとやすみしよう

When you're tired, take a break.

たっぷり眠ったり

Get plenty of sleep,

おしゃべりしたり

...talk with friends,

美味しいものを
食べたり

...eat something tasty,

そうして元気になったら
またかわいい笑顔を見せてね

...and when you're feeling better,
show me that cute smile again.

君の笑顔は
世界を幸せにする

*Your smile makes the world
a happier place.*

いつだって、
どんな君だって、
ぎゅっと抱きしめるよ

No matter what,
I will always be here to
give you a big hug.

そのぬくもりは、やさしさは

The warmth and kindness,

わたしから、君へ
…from me to you,

君から、誰かへ

...from you to someone else,

つらなって、輪になって
...connecting and forming a circle.

きっと広がっていく
It will surely spread

時を超えて
...through time,

世代を超えて

いつか地球を抱きしめる

...until one day, it hugs the entire Earth.

君は大切な宝物

You are a
precious treasure.

ぎゅっと抱きしめて

That's why I'll always be here to give you a big hug.

大好きだよ

I love you.

この本に登場するディズニー作品
the Disney Works in This Book.

『アナと雪の女王』 Frozen

『アナと雪の女王2』 Frozen2

『アラジン』 Aladdin

『インサイド・ヘッド2』 Inside Out2

『カーズ』 Cars

『カールじいさんの空飛ぶ家』 Up

『くまのプーさん』 Winnie the Pooh

『ジャングル・ブック』
The Jungle Book

『シュガー・ラッシュ：オンライン』
Ralph Breaks the Internet :
Wreck-It Ralph2

『白雪姫』
Snow White and the
Seven Dwarfs

『シンデレラ』 Cinderella

『ズートピア』 Zootopia

『ダンボ』 Dumbo

『トイ・ストーリー2』 Toy Story2

『トイ・ストーリー3』 Toy Story3

『トイ・ストーリー4』 Toy Story4

『塔の上のラプンツェル』 Tangled

『ノートルダムの鐘』
The Hunchback of Notre Dame

『ピーター・パン』 Peter Pan

『ピノキオ』 Pinocchio

『美女と野獣』
Beauty and the Beast

『ファインディング・ドリー』
Finding Dory

『プリンセスと魔法のキス』
The Princess and the Frog

『ベイマックス』 Big Hero6

『マイ・エレメント』 Elemental

『魔法使いの弟子』
The Sorcerer's Apprentice
（『ファンタジア』より）

『ムーラン』 Mulan

『モアナと伝説の海』 Moana

『モアナと伝説の海2』 Moana2

『モンスターズ・インク』
Monsters, Inc.

『ライオン・キング』
The Lion King

『リトル・マーメイド』
The Little Mermaid

『リロ＆スティッチ』 Lilo & Stitch

『レミーのおいしいレストラン』
Ratatouille

Disney 抱きしめたい

Everything I Need to Know about Love I Learned from Disney

2024 年 11 月 26 日　第 1 刷発行
2025 年 7 月 7 日　第 2 刷発行

構成・編集……講談社
文………………李 正美
装丁……………吉田優子（Well Planning）
発行者…………安永尚人
発行所…………株式会社講談社
　　　　　　　〒112-8001　東京都文京区音羽 2-12-21
電話……………編集　03-5395-3142
　　　　　　　販売　03-5395-3625
　　　　　　　業務　03-5395-3615
印刷所…………共同印刷株式会社
製本所…………大口製本印刷株式会社

KODANSHA

ISBN978-4-06-536994-4　Printed in Japan　N.D.C.778 95p 24cm
©2024 Disney　©2024 Disney/Pixar　©Disney. Based on the "Winnie the Pooh" works by A.A. Milne and E.H. Shepard.
©Just Play, LLC.
Mr. Potato Head® and *Mrs. Potato Head*® are registered trademarks of Hasbro,Inc. Used with permission. ©Hasbro,Inc. All rights reserved.

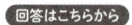

この本についての
ご感想を
お聞かせください。

回答はこちらから